M000282216

HOW TO GO TO CONFESSION
WHEN YOU DON'T KNOW HOW

ANN M.S. LEBLANC

ST. ANTHONY MESSENGER PRESS

Cincinnati, Ohio

Nihil Obstat:	Donald Miller, O.F.M.
	Rev. Richard W. Walling
Imprimi Potest:	Fred Link, O.F.M.
	Provincial
Imprimatur:	+Most Rev. Carl K. Moeddel, V.G.
	Archdiocese of Cincinnati
	January 2, 2003

The *nihil obstat* and *imprimatur* are a declaration that a book or pamphlet is considered to be free from doctrinal or moral error. It is not implied that those who have granted the *nihil obstat* and *imprimatur* agree with the contents, opinions or statements expressed.

Scripture citations are taken from the *New Revised Standard Version Bible*, copyright ©1989 by the Division of Christian Education of the National Council of Churches of Christ in the U.S.A. and used by permission.

LIBRARY OF CONGRESS CATALOGING-IN-PUBLICATION DATA

LeBlanc, Ann M. S., 1952-
  How to go to confession when you don't know how / Ann M.S. LeBlanc.
     p. cm.
  ISBN 0-86716-521-9 (pbk.)
  1. Confession (Liturgy)—Catholic Church. 2. Catholic
Church—Liturgy. I. Title.
  BX2265.3.L43 2003
  264'.02086—dc21

                                   2002155147

Cover and book design by Mark Sullivan
Cover photo by Gene Plaisted, O.S.C.

ISBN-13: 978-0-86716-521-0
ISBN-10: 0-86716-521-9

Copyright ©2003, Ann M.S. LeBlanc

Published by St. Anthony Messenger Press
28 W. Liberty St.
Cincinnati, OH 45202
www.AmericanCatholic.org

Printed on acid-free paper

Printed in the U.S.A.

                    06 07 08 09 10 5 4 3 2

for

FATHER JOHN AUDIBERT,
FATHER RALPH BOISVERT—
priests, teachers, friends

.

· CONTENTS

This book is about celebrating the sacrament of reconciliation by making an appointment to meet with a priest specifically for that purpose. It isn't about standing in line before Mass on Saturday afternoon. I wouldn't have the faintest idea how to celebrate the sacrament that way, not having done it since I was a kid. Also, since returning to Catholicism after a long absence, I've had the privilege of being able to have reconciliation mostly with a priest who knows me very, very well, Father John. I don't know what it would be like to do this with someone that I don't know at all. Our parish, while large for our area, is still small compared to those in big cities. It's easy to get to know our priests personally. While this book probably won't speak to people who prefer anonymity during reconciliation, it is offered as a bridge to those looking for a way back to this sacrament, to peace and healing.

CHAPTER ONE

Do You Go to Confession?

On returning
to Catholicism after a thirty-year absence, this was the
most common question that I was asked. Oh, not right
away, and usually after a few preliminary feelers, but it
almost always came up eventually: "Do you go to confession?" Sometimes the real question was, "Do they still
have confession?" Other times it was, "Do you, a not-
particularly-humble (one might even say arrogant), person actually recognize, much less acknowledge your failings out loud to another person?" Often the unspoken
words were, "Isn't it horrible?" or "I could never do that."

And, of course, there were the stories from childhood. Stories about lying in confession, then confessing
to lying. Some made up sins to confess because their
actual failings were insufficient. Others had a list that
they confessed every time, regardless of what had actually been going on: "I talked back to my mother three
times said a bad word twice and stole a piece of chalk
from the blackboard once that's all Father. Oh, and I
lied once." Some remembered the kids in line who actually wrote down lists to read from. Everyone knew that
the time spent in the confessional was of critical importance. Too little time and everyone knew that you lied;

too much time and everybody wondered what you had been up to.

Some of the best confessions were the practice ones with Sister Mary (insert saint's name here) before the all-important first confession. Whole classes of murdering, embezzling, hubcap-stealing second graders 'fessed up to their foul deeds while learning the routine for the real event: "Bless me, Sister, unh, Father, this is my first confession. I killed my sister once, stole a million dollars and watched TV twice after I was supposed to be in bed. That's all, Father . . . ah . . . Sister . . . Father." These snapshots of our tiny grade school psyches must have led thousands of nuns to lay their heads on their desks in convulsive laughter, or in prayers of thanksgiving that we were too small to act on our impulses.

Everyone has some version of "The Priest Who Fell Asleep," "The Priest Who Talked Real Loud," "How to Get the Priest Who Gave Easy Penances" and "How Me and My Friend Harold Tried to Sneak Up and Hear Carole Ellen Plante's Confession to See if She Was Really Fast Like Eddie Moore Said She Was." Popular among boys is the "The Time the Priest Got Really Mad at Me." Girls had more versions of "How Much I Worried That I Forgot Something and Would Go *Straight to Hell* if I Got Hit by a Truck."

By the time junior high came around, sins against purity rose to the confessional Top Ten list, although plenty of kids had apparently been routinely confessing them for years with no idea what they were. The rush of hormones clarified this matter considerably, inspiring new waves of creativity in the confessional and tortured anxiety the rest of the time. New techniques, such as "How to Say 'Masturbation' without Really Saying It," and new questions, such as "Is French Kissing an Impure Act if You Really Didn't Feel Anything?" came to the fore. New stories included "The Priest Who Asked a Lot of Questions" and "The Priest Who Asked a *Real* Lot of Questions."

Most stories were amused, affectionate memories of childhood antics and worries, of harried, tolerant priests trying to do their best. Some were genuinely awful memories of hurt and bewilderment. These were never recounted in detail and didn't lend themselves to funny titles. They were alluded to in the eyes-averted, hushed-voice tones of real pain and of continuing humiliation. These were the stories of being shamed and berated in the confessional, of fear and of anger. In tight-lipped bitterness, in sadness and with firm resolution, these allusions came with the spoken or unspoken message, "That will never happen to me again."

Most people who asked, "Do you go to confession?" counted themselves as "fallen away," "lapsed" or "recovering" Catholics. I eventually realized that many who considered themselves to be active Catholics did not ask this question for one reason: they do not participate in the sacrament of reconciliation. While the whole matter of confession can be a matter of intense curiosity, explicit distress or just great stories for those who no longer practice, it is a matter of considerable anxiety for many of those who do. They find themselves in a tight bind, eager to practice their faith but avoiding this most personal of sacraments.

For active and inactive Catholics alike, the anxiety peeking out from the blanket of humor, the anger and fear of those hurt in the past, the worry and self-consciousness, all make it difficult to find the healing and mercy so central to our faith. Beginning to think about reconciliation is the first step in getting over our distress about confession.

CHAPTER TWO

Reconciliation

When Father John first mentioned the sacrament of reconciliation to me, I thought, "Wow. They even invented a new sacrament while I was gone." Once he had clarified the situation, my next thought was, "I've got to throw up," followed by, "I'm outta' here." Actually, I made a statement, many statements, over weeks and weeks, mostly involving how I was never going to do this again, how I was not going to be in any religion that involved this kind of brutalizing, stupid practice, ever, no way, no how, thank you very much, goodbye. Those weeks of conversations could be pretty much characterized as follows:

> "I'm not going to do it."
>
> "You don't have to, Ann."
>
> "No way I'm going to do it."
>
> "You don't have to, Ann."
>
> "No *!%*!& way I'm going to do it."
>
> "No one can make you, Ann."
>
> "It's not going to happen, so you can forget it!"
>
> "That's all right, Ann."
>
> "I'm not going to do it!"
>
> "Will you *listen* to yourself?"

Was I one of those people who had had a Bad Experience in confession? Oh, yes. Was I going to get over it? Not if I could help it.

Father John, having been around the track a few times, began to talk about reconciliation. Not *reconciliation*, certainly not the *sacrament of reconciliation*, just reconciliation. I don't remember that he even used the word *reconciliation* at first, since it tended to lead to condensed, colorful versions of the dialogue above. Sometimes, we would just sit quietly for a while, time that I needed to calm myself. We talked about a lot of things, and even got around to gingerly touching on The Bad Experience. We sat quietly quite a lot. I began to experience safety and assurance. I began to feel cared for and accepted.

I began to experience reconciliation.

Long before we ever celebrated the sacrament of reconciliation, we celebrated compassion. In Father John's gentleness and sense of humor, I began to recognize God's mercy, to accept God's touch and to allow the gradual softening of my heart. It was as though, for a long time, Father John would hold this gift out to me on an open palm, or sometimes wordlessly set it on the arm of my chair. Sometimes I would ignore it. Sometimes I would pick it up and turn it around, looking at the outside. Occasionally I would ask him to untie the string. A few times I unexpectedly took off more of the wrapping than I intended and got a little panicked. He carefully took it from me, wrapped it up and set it on the arm of my chair again. He would smile a little, and say, "It's alright, Ann." He probably said "It's alright, Ann," a thousand times. I was learning about God, about God's compassion and tolerance and forgiveness, through the compassion and tolerance and forgiveness of a human being. I was learning that it really was all right.

In gradually coming to recognize how God enfolded me, I began to see that this was of itself a healing. I began to understand that God had already given me the gift, and all I had to do was unwrap it.

Did I unwrap it? Nope. Was I going to do it? No way, no how, not ever, no thanks, see you later, 'bye. I had been learning about reconciliation, but when I thought about it, the automatic find/replace function of my consciousness inserted *confession* for every occurrence of *reconciliation*. Smooth reptiles whispered, "Bad experience!" in my ear, and every neuron in my body screamed, "Run! Run for your life!" God's part of reconciliation sounded pretty good, but the practical human details were too awful to think about.

Of course, I thought about them all the time. Could I do this with Father John, or would it have to be with some other priest? Would I have to go in one of those little rooms? What would I say? How could I be sure that nothing bad would happen? What would I say? What would he say? What would I say? Could you do it wrong? What would I say? Father John had explained this already, probably two or three times, but I find that it's hard to listen when your neurons are running for their lives, and any religion without this sacrament is looking better all the time. I never did get the gory details straightened out, until one day, heart in my throat, I said, "I wonder if we could have reconciliation?" and Father John said, "Yes. Yes, we could."

CHAPTER THREE

The Not-So-Gory Details

Although Father John had taken plenty of time to prepare me to actually celebrate the sacrament of reconciliation, when we finally got to this place, I was so nervous, I couldn't have figured out how to make a peanut butter sandwich. Priests are used to this and are good at helping us muddle through. For me, it was tremendously reassuring to be sitting in an office that I knew, with a person that I trusted and with whom I had already talked about private things. I was relieved to find out that I didn't have to go in any little room. I could take all the time I needed to figure out what I was going to say with no line of impatient parishioners waiting for me to be finished. Most importantly, Father John would coach me, and I couldn't do it wrong.

Here's what happens:
1. You go in and sit down and talk about all the usual things you normally talk about when you meet someone. The priest expects you to be nervous and tries to help you feel at ease. If you already know him, this is easy. If you don't already know each other, you probably talk about your life situation, what kind of work you do, your relationships and

things that will help the priest know a little about who you are. There isn't any secret formula that you have to memorize.

2. The priest might read something from the Bible to help you both focus your attention on God's forgiveness and mercy. You don't absolutely have to do this, but it really helped me the first time, especially. You can select the reading and read it yourself, if you prefer.

3. You pray. You ask God to be with you and help you to be open to God's healing.

4. You talk about your sins, the failings that you've had, the things that you've done that you're not so proud of, the things that you didn't do that you should have, the nastier attitudes that you have, the ways that you might have hurt people and the times that you turned away from God. You don't have to go down any official list of sins to see if you've committed any—most of us have a pretty clear idea of where we've messed up. The priest mostly listens quietly. Sometimes he'll ask you to clarify something or say something to help you along. It doesn't all have to be deathly serious. Sometimes you both end up laughing, or sometimes the priest even tells you something about himself. Sometimes you might cry a little. Don't worry about it—people cry all the time during this part and the priest has tissues handy. They probably have a whole course on tissues in seminary. Eventually, you kind of know when you've come to the end of what you're going to talk about for that

time. You want to talk about all the major failings that you're aware of, but you don't have to obsess about every tiny detail. The priest will help you if you're not sure.

5. You and the priest talk about it. You agree on something that you can do to further this reconciliation. This could be some action, some kind of reparation or sacrifice, prayers, good deeds—usually things that will help you be more thoughtful about areas of sinfulness or failing, or things that will help you do better about turning to God. This is called the penance. It apparently used to always be "two Our Father's and one Hail Mary," but we're more creative now. The idea is to really try to decide on something that will challenge you a little.

6. You pray some more, asking God to forgive you. You resolve to do better. The priest prays and offers you God's forgiveness. This is called absolution.

7. You thank God for his mercy and compassion.

8. You and the priest probably talk about how this went, and he tries to encourage you. It's nice if you tell the priest about the things that he did or said that were especially helpful for you and if you thank him. This isn't exactly the easiest thing in the world for priests, either.

9. If the priest is someone you know, you probably talk about other things. When you leave, though, you end up thinking about what you talked about and

making plans for how you're going to do better, how to do what you decided on for penance.

CHAPTER FOUR

Questions People Ask and Some I Made Up

How long does it take?
I'm not telling. If I say five minutes, you'll think I was lying. If I say an hour, you'll wonder what I've been up to. Don't be surprised if it takes you a half an hour or so sometimes, though. The nice thing about making an appointment is that you and the priest can really talk about what's going on and how you want to try to change.

Isn't it embarrassing if you have to talk about sex?
Yes.

I'm afraid some of the things I have to talk about will shock the priest.
One of the great myths of Catholicism is that priests are sheltered hothouse flowers. They aren't. Well, at least parish priests aren't. They have chosen to live with, work with, listen to and help us with every imaginable kind of problem. There isn't much they haven't heard, seen or had to figure out. You can pretty much guarantee that unless your priest never did anything but go to school he has stories that would make you faint. He probably has to be careful not to shock *you*.

Isn't it embarrassing to see the priest to whom you told all these personal things later, like on the golf course?
No. Well, not unless his game is really bad.

I've heard that reconciliation is like therapy.
The people who say this are usually slightly grandiose therapists who've never been to confession. *Reconciliation is nothing like therapy.* Nothing against therapy, I've had plenty and done plenty. Nowhere in therapy do you step into the arms of God. Most therapists would actually frown on this. Also—dare I say it?—while most therapists are very nice, competent persons, they aren't priests. The whole idea of God makes a lot of them very nervous. As a result, therapy tends to stay in a certain box, whereas the sacrament of reconciliation blows up the box, makes it irrelevant, uninteresting and kind of restricting.

How often are you supposed to do it?
You're supposed to do it once a year. Naturally, if you're conscious of serious sin, it's better to celebrate reconciliation right away. Personally, I think once a year is a little skimpy, but when you consider that some Catholics don't do it at all, I guess that's the bottom line. I found that, when I was first getting the hang of it, there were things I wanted to talk about in reconciliation every two or three months. A lot of people find it especially helpful during Advent and again during Lent. This would be a good thing to talk about with the priest with whom you celebrate the sacrament. Myself, I find that

when I start feeling ticked off and irritable all the time, critical of everyone around me, nasty toward my husband and prone to using four-letter words (okay, okay, Father John: *more than usual),* there's probably something I need to look at, own up to or let go of, and reconciliation helps me do that.

What if I just don't have anything to talk about in reconciliation?
Ha! Ha! Ha!

I haven't practiced as a Catholic in fifteen years! How am I supposed to remember every bad thing I've ever done?
Relax! Relax! You don't have to! The idea is to talk about the big chunks, especially in this situation. Later, you can spend more time looking at specific things, but the first time you want to do more of a general survey. There are probably a few things that are really weighing on you, and it's good to get to those right away.

Even abortion?
Run, do not walk, to the sacrament of reconciliation. Women who are struggling with an abortion in their past have come to expect judgment and condemnation. Sometimes the harshest voices are their own. Yet, there cannot exist many parish priests who have not sat quietly and compassionately as hundreds of women sobbed their hearts out about abortions. It may be that your first conversation will be about the weather, about changes in the parish or about the adult faith formation

classes. Maybe your second conversation will focus a little more on your faith and your personal history. Take the time that you need to feel safe. When you and the priest build this trusting groundwork, the deepest disclosures can be made more completely and honestly. This is nothing to rush into, and you should be ready to hold nothing back. You'll probably find what thousands of women already know: that parish priests understand human pain.

I just confess my sins right to God. Isn't that just as good?
I don't know—maybe for God, but probably not for you. I have to tell you that there is something incredibly powerful and healing about saying the words out loud to another person who is intent on helping you experience God's mercy. Most people that I've talked with who think that confessing their sins right to God is just as good as the sacrament of reconciliation haven't celebrated the sacrament of reconciliation lately. Most people who celebrate the sacrament of reconciliation regularly are very clear that they have plenty of personal conversations with God in the living room, out in the yard, in the car and so forth, often about their numerous failings, but that they would not consider these an adequate substitute for the sacrament of reconciliation.

What if our priest is a dud at reconciliation?
Well, it's always possible that your priest is a dud, in which case, you can shop around and try to find some-

one with whom you feel more comfortable. On the other hand, maybe the day you went, his cat had died, the parish council was complaining about the Mass schedule *again*, and it looked like somebody was stealing cold cuts from the soup kitchen icebox. Maybe you were so nervous that he thought he was doing a lousy job and that made *him* nervous. Maybe he was trying to give up smoking. Who knows? Some days, I'm a dud myself. It's probably worth going back, talking about what you experienced and checking it out with him. Most priests, like most people, aren't duds most of the time. I'm not saying this would be easy, but you might be surprised.

CHAPTER FIVE

Sin as a Heart Condition

I have no idea how they do it these days, but I have clear memories of official lists of sins, mortal sins, venial sins, cardinal sins. That is to say, I remember the lists, but couldn't tell you what was on them. There are Web pages devoted to these topics, apparently for people who are getting ready for the sacrament of reconciliation and don't want to miss any teeny tiny sin they might have committed. If you're looking for official lists and definitions, don't look here, because I don't have any. I'm a garden-variety Catholic fumbling around like everybody else, not an expert on sin. (Well, only a few kinds of sin!) Most of us don't need a checklist to figure out what parts of our lives are less than exemplary—we worry about them, we try to do better, we try to hide them from ourselves and others. A list can help us begin to look at ourselves honestly, but eventually, we need to go further.

It does seem like adults examining their lives and thinking about reconciliation these days are likely also to ask themselves "Have I been dishonest?" as well as "Have I lied? Have I stolen?" People are trying to examine their attitudes as much as their behavior looking at questions of integrity and of charity, on conditions of the heart:

- · Have I hurt others by my actions or words?

- · Have I shown patience and understanding with my spouse, my children, my colleagues at work?

- · Have I built myself up by talking against someone else?

- · Have I offered a helping hand to a struggling employee, to a confused person in the grocery store, to a mother with a screaming toddler? Or have I turned away?

- · Have I turned to God with my pain, frustration and disappointment? Or have I turned away?

- · Have I turned to God in joy and gratitude? Or have I ignored him at these times?

- · Have I treated the gift of my body with respect and care?

- · Have I been stingy or generous with my time, money, energy, love?

- · Have pride or anger contaminated my life, my relationships with others and with God?

- · How much does greed rule my life? Do I worry more about things than about people?

- · Do I turn to God every day?

- · How do I cherish those around me?

Instead of checking off lists, we find ourselves responding to Jesus' radical challenge to go beyond the rules, to love even when it seems impossible, to give more than we can afford, to bear more than we think we can. He asks us to leap recklessly off the ledge of commitment, to trust when it seems that we've been abandoned, to empty ourselves in God's service. In the face of all that, a confession like "I missed Mass on Sunday once, I yelled at my husband ten times, I swore five times and I thought about having sex with my accountant twice" starts to seem like a good beginning but maybe not the whole story.

How about:

> "You know, Father, it seems like I don't give anybody a chance anymore. My kid left his bike on the walk and I ranted and raved at him for half an hour. My secretary left the cover sheet off a stack of draft proposals, and I slammed them on her desk and snapped at her. I don't know what it is—everything gets to me and the next thing you know I'm mad and saying things to put people down."

> "I just gave up. I had prayed and prayed and when I didn't get the job, I told God to go to hell. I haven't prayed or gone to Mass in a year and, every chance I get, I tell people that religion is a crock."

> "After the rape, I felt filthy. I slept with guys I didn't even like and it made me feel worse, and, well . . . it got to the point where I hate myself and everybody else."

> "I knew she was sensitive about her weight and I knew that if I said something she'd leave me alone, and to be honest, I was sick of her always hanging around my desk like some little puppy dog. She disgusts me, actually, and she smells."

We also struggle with things that we know are on the official list of *extremely bad sins* but with which we struggle in our conscience. These are the issues that challenge our consciences and our relationships with each other, with the church and with God. Surprise, surprise, s-e-x is often involved. Do we use contraception? Is masturbation still a sin? Can we have sexual interactions in loving nonmarital relationships? How do we reestablish ourselves in marriage after divorce? Who decides? How do we decide? What are the official church teachings? Why do there seem to be so many unofficial practices?

What can I tell you? If you're struggling with decisions you've made or are trying to make, there's a place to talk about it.

Andy and Sarah, for example, had decided as young teachers that they wanted between 1.6 and 2.4 children based on their estimated income, the time that they would want to devote to each child and so forth. They decided that two complete children would be best and thought that three years apart would be nice. A year and a half after Hillary was born, Josh was conceived, despite much careful observation of charts, temperatures and mucus, and Andy's bad jokes about the bedroom being more like a lab than a love nest. They were both too excited to quibble about the timing, though, and Josh was eagerly welcomed.

Two and a half years later, when Mikey was born, Andy joked that all that birds and bees stuff was wrong and that babies came from sharing toothbrushes. Sarah was getting a little sick of Andy's jokes, however, and worried contantly. They talked and talked about it and, finally, Andy got his tubes tied, so to speak. Shared toothbrushes or not, they were permanently a family of five. This was just fine with Andy.

Sarah, on the other hand, had expected to feel relieved, but found herself feeling distressed and, let's face it, not quite right in bed. She didn't think she should even be receiving communion, but avoided reconciliation because she knew that, given the situation, she couldn't honestly say that she was sorry they had taken the route that they did. When Hillary made her first communion, Sarah felt like such a hypocrite that she cried all night. After a while, she stayed home on Sunday mornings more often than not, telling Andy that she really needed to get dinner ready if his parents were coming over, that Mike needed some of her time to himself or that she just didn't feel well. Eventually, it was just as easy for Andy to stay home, too, and they sort of drifted away.

Now, fifteen years later, Sarah and Andy consider themselves Catholic, and faithfully attend Mass on Christmas and Easter. They don't believe that they have done anything wrong, but they know that in the eyes of the church they have. They see the "Catholics Can Always Come Home" signs and brochures, but don't think these apply to them.

I would love to write, "Then Sarah and Andy decided to have reconciliation, and everything turned out fine, and they lived happy Catholic lives forever after," but I can't. A dozen different priests would handle this a dozen different ways in reconciliation, and maybe one of them would leave Sarah or Andy more confused than ever. The idea is that both Sarah and Andy could bring their thoughts about this to reconciliation. They could also set up some time to talk about it with their priest, together or separately. They could begin to look honestly at how they had made this decision, trying to progress in their understanding, accepting the invitation to grow offered through the sacrament. Sometimes we all do our best, struggling alone with complicated moral decisions, past and present. Often we avoid talking to those who would suggest a course of action different from what we want to do. Sometimes we talk ourselves into sin. Later, sometimes years later, we can come to harsh conclusions, forgetting that God's mercy is always close at hand. As Catholics, we never have to go it alone.

When I've brought tricky, upsetting things like this to reconciliation, I've ended up learning about what the church teaches is the ideal thing to do, talking about how I came to my decision, about how I feel about it now, what I wish I had done differently, what I feel totally fine about and what it all means in terms of how I act now. I've talked about decisions or actions that I was totally comfortable with, but which I knew were not according to what the church taught. My theory was that I should at least put it out there to be completely honest and not pretend that I didn't know that there could be an issue. Imagine my surprise on finding that I came away peacefully, even when I had been helped to see the self-deception in matters about which I had previously been assertively, even aggressively "okay." I've gained a greater sense of honesty about myself and a step closer to the truth. Sometimes, I've had to face unattractive things that I had tucked away beneath a certain excessive confidence about decisions or behavior. Sometimes, I've been helped to see that I was not as evil as I thought.

No kidding.

CHAPTER SIX

Before and After

When I first
began to celebrate the sacrament of reconciliation, I
would just wing it. I knew that most people probably
planned out what they were going to talk about, but
this was just too nerve-wracking for me. Since there
wasn't a line of people waiting, I had plenty of time to
figure out what to say and no shortage of failures to
pick from. I'd just start at the top of the list and work
my way down, sort of haphazardly. This actually
worked just fine.

What I discovered in rather short order was that reconciliation was not an end point. Instead, I had stepped
into a process that stretched infinitely ahead and
included self-examination, prayer, celebration of the
Eucharist, penance and reconciliation as parts of a
dynamic continuum. Gradually, I began to spend a few
minutes at the end of each day looking back on where
I had done well and where I had faltered. This reflection
eventually became the first moments of a time of daily
prayer and a fertile source of self-understanding that I
could bring to the sacrament of reconciliation.

Most people are amazed at how good they feel after
reconciliation. Some have talked about feeling clean, as

though they have a new start. Others feel exhilarated or energized, ready to take on the world. Many describe feelings of deep peace, or of a lightness and freedom. After the first time, I wrote to Father John:

> It made me feel as though I were stand-
> ing in a stiff breeze with new skin, like a
> clean culvert with a torrent of spring
> rain running through, like a dried-out
> sponge tossed in the ocean. It felt like
> connections long dead were alive again,
> as though light and power could run
> through me unimpeded. For a little
> while, all I have to do is close my eyes,
> breathe and accept God's touch.

These feelings of renewal lead you to think about how to carry this reconciliation into the rest of your life. In agreeing on a penance, you've already identified one small step. This could be something as simple as sitting quietly in gratitude for a few minutes a day or turning off the TV during supper. It could be as complicated as arranging your schedule so that you get home no later than a certain time each day. These practices, small and large, lend themselves to moments of reflection, espe-cially during the time that you've agreed to do them. In contrast to the "two Our Father's, one Hail Mary" approach, you have a period of time in which you're likely to be more conscious than usual about some behavior, or thought pattern, or attitude that you'd like to change. You think about it. You pay attention to how you're doing. You become more aware of when you slip and when you succeed.

Cara, for example, had become aware that she had hardly any patience with the older members of her work team, who had limited computer skills and no apparent interest in gaining any. She knew that some of her frustration came out as hurtful remarks, leading one coworker to leave a meeting in tears. In reconciliation Father Ed suggested that she try to find the opportunity to compliment one member of the work team on one computer-related accomplishment per day for a couple of weeks. Cara doubted that this would be possible, since there were days that turning on the computers seemed to be a challenge for her team, but agreed to give it a try.

The closest Cara came the first day was complimenting Dorothy on her blouse while she was in the process of botching up a simple data entry task. Cara thought that, if worse came to worse, she could at least say nice things to her coworkers while they were in the vicinity of computers. This is what she did for another couple of days. On the fourth day, Hal actually produced an intact document and Cara was so genuinely delighted that she really poured it on. Hal smiled proudly to himself as he deleted the template that he needed for the next document, but somehow this didn't seem as disastrous as it could have. Dorothy remembered that she had an earlier version of the template and life went on. In the process of trying to find successes in her team, Cara found herself doing some coaching, some cheerleading and a bit more laughing, sometimes at herself. When mistakes were made, and they were made by the dozen, she could express her frustration loudly and sometimes with colorful language, but somehow the biting edge was gone. The team seemed to relax a little, and by the end of the two weeks, Cara noticed that she was exceeding her one-a-day compliment quota.

Cara also noticed that members of the team seemed to have more good ideas than they had before, although usually not related to computers. Dorothy was a whiz at organizing accounts, and Hal had very useful informal connections with his counterparts on other work teams. Another member turned out to have some advertising background, which he put to good use in suggesting ways to organize their reports. As she took a few minutes each evening to review her day, Cara started to realize that, although her work team probably had the crummiest computer skills in the company, the chip on her own shoulder had kept them from using the other skills that they did have. While there were still plenty of days in which she had to struggle not to say something awful, and some days that she failed miserably, it seemed that both she and her team were able to take each others' failings more in stride. More importantly, they were all able to celebrate their mutual successes.

The next time Cara saw Father Ed for reconciliation, she talked not about her snappishness, which she now saw as the tip of the iceberg, but about her tendency to take her own uncertainties and anxieties as a young team leader out on others.

What can happen in the process of reconciliation is a gradual opening of the heart, a conversion to new ways of living. As we take the time to look gently and honestly at ourselves, every day, every week or just every so often, in the spirit of the sacrament of reconciliation, we find that it's not as awful as we expected. Like Cara, we might pick up one end of a thread when we confess our sins, follow that thread in the weeks or months afterward as part of penance and find ourselves talking about a new level of understanding when we come to the sacrament again. We begin to see connections, we begin to look a little deeper, we begin to hold ourselves to a little higher standard. We know that as we set the bar higher, we will often fail to get over it, especially at first.

Having experienced God's mercy in a very practical way, however, we find it a little easier to forgive ourselves. In that same mercy, we find the strength to try again and again. As reconciliation becomes part of the texture of our lives, we discover challenge as well as forgiveness, strength as well as healing.

Chapter Seven

Opening to God

In my "no way, no how, not ever, even if hell freezes over" phase about the sacrament of reconciliation, I figured that, since I was so special, it would be just fine with God if I had my own little private sacrament of reconciliation, just me and God, no middleman. Even then, however, I was able to recognize a basic falseness in this plan. Something was missing. It turns out that there's something vitally important about the middleman, the other human, the priest.

In books about reconciliation, the priest is often discussed as communicating God's mercy in human, tangible ways. Confession to a priest is discussed as symbolic of the communal nature of this sacrament, of how sin distances us from our community, and how in reconciliation, we move toward healing those gaps. There seems to be another part to it, though, something that is probably a little more nerve-wracking to think about.

In reconciliation, we are taking a risk, on a human level, at least. If we approach the sacrament sincerely, we know that we are going to make ourselves extremely vulnerable in front of another person. We can read and think and talk all we want about how that other person represents Christ, but on a practical level, we are about to talk about the most private parts of our lives, perhaps with someone that we might not know all that well. Sometimes it seems more difficult to talk about these things with someone that we do know pretty well. We're going to let the protective layers and facades fall away, and some we will need to peel off intentionally. We are going to make ourselves entirely open. We will sometimes feel shame or embarrassment; we might become tearful; we will sometimes feel awkward or uncertain. We will experience the natural human feelings that we have about our less attractive behavior.

When we talk about confessing directly to God, I wonder how much we are really saying, "I don't want to feel those uncomfortable feelings." Confessing directly to God, nice, abstract Being that he is, bypasses all the messy interpersonal aspects of dealing with another human. It has the extra, added advantage that God already knows our transgressions, in detail, and so we don't actually have to say the words out loud and hear ourselves saying them. We can be pretty sure that God won't be asking us any questions, either. All in all, when we talk about confessing directly to God, we can pretend that we're clinging to noble ideals, while at the same time keeping things neat, clean and comfortable for ourselves. We can tell ourselves that we can be much more open with God directly, but we're actually avoiding some of the meaning of our failings.

When we decide wholeheartedly to seek reconciliation, we are deciding to lay ourselves open completely before God. Part of that completeness includes the interpersonal discomfort of laying ourselves open before another human being. The priest sees our eyes as we talk, and we see his. The priest is aware of our awkwardness, and we receive his encouragement. We stumble in our account and are helped to continue. We laugh ruefully about shared experience and find our own pain reflected in the priest's words. There's nothing easy about it. We are acknowledging that healing requires not only that God know our failings, but that we also confront them in their every manifestation. In reconciliation, we face not only the sin but the anxiety, the fear, the shame and the pain. As humans, we experience this best in interaction with others. As Catholics, we agree not to wiggle away from it.

Most of the time we manage to choke out the more uncomfortable things that we have to talk about in reconciliation without fainting. There are probably even a few people who love tearfully going over, in painful detail, their every humiliating transgression. The rest of us, however, have moments when doing a root canal on ourselves without anesthesia would be preferable to confession.

Here are some ideas:

> Try saying, "Well, Father, I think I'd rather do a root canal on myself without an anesthetic than talk with you about this . . ." This gives the priest a chance to help you out. Reconciliation is not the best place to try out comedy rou-

tines, but a little touch of humor can help ease your anxiety. It lets the priest know that you're upset but not near meltdown.

Before reconciliation, think about the things that you want to talk about and identify any difficulty that you might have. Some things might not bother you to talk about at all, some might cause embarrassment, some could lead to anxiety and so forth. The idea here is to think about it a little beforehand so that you aren't surprised when the moment comes.

Sometimes you might need to say something like, "I want to talk about something here, Father, but I'm not sure how to say it, and I guess I'd like to try and just get it out and if you have any questions about it, maybe you could just ask at the end?" No matter how garbled you get this message, the priest will understand it. They know that sometimes you just have to stumble your way through the whole story.

It helps to be specific about the worries that you have. If Father Peabody yelled at you when you were ten and everybody outside could hear, and now you always think it's going to happen again, tell the priest about it. If you have something really uncomfortable to confess, and you're worried about how to act the next time you see the priest after Mass, talk about it. If you hate to cry in front of people, but you're pretty sure you're going to, and it will only upset you more, let him know. There is no one more expert than priests at helping people manage awkward situations, worries and fears.

At the end, talk about how it all went. Saying something like "That wasn't as bad as I expected" helps you and the priest realize that things went okay. Even saying, "Whew! That was awful!" helps open the door to talking about what was difficult for you, how you and the priest might approach the sacrament next time, or what you might want to think about in the meantime. The idea here is to acknowledge that you are two human beings trying your best to be open to God's grace, even when it's not easy or comfortable.

As an example, Paul is a thirty-six-year-old restaurant owner who has been married about ten years. He and his wife Sheila have two children and would both say that they have a successful, happy marriage. In the last couple of years, though, Paul has found himself spending a few hours a week visiting pornographic Web sites and masturbating often enough that he doesn't approach Sheila to make love as much as she would like. She hasn't said anything, but Paul can tell that she's wondering if anything is going on.

Sheila and Paul attend Mass at St. Maximilian's most Sundays, and they have participated in the Lenten Penitential Service for the last several years. Last year Paul couldn't bring himself to talk about the porn sites and the masturbating, remembering how all the boys in his class had been taken aside for a special fire-and-brimstone lecture about sex in eighth grade. He had never talked about this in confession as a kid and wasn't about to start now. On the other hand, he was aware that he had a problem starting and had felt lousy about making what he saw as a bad confession last year.

Finally, after Father Jim gave a pretty down-to-earth homily one Sunday, Paul made an appointment to see him. He didn't say what it was for, figuring he could make something up for a quick getaway if he had to. When he sat down with Father Jim, however, he found himself blurting out that he had something really embarrassing for reconciliation, and that he didn't think he could actually do it, that he was afraid of what Father Jim would think of him, but that it was starting to wear him down and he didn't know what to do. Father Jim sat quietly for a few seconds, then asked, "Do you think you'd like to celebrate the sacrament of reconciliation now, or would you just like to talk about what's on your mind first?" They talked about this for a while, and Paul realized that he would be able to talk just as easily in the sacrament of reconciliation.

When they started, Father Jim talked a little bit about what it's like for two people to walk over rough terrain together, and how it helps if one person has already been down that path. Paul began to talk, but couldn't go on, turning his eyes away and sitting silently for a long time. Father Jim asked him if he could ask a question, and Paul said that it would be all right. When Father Jim asked him what had started bothering Paul so much about this failing that he had made an appointment, Paul began to talk about how he saw himself hurting Sheila and his relationship with her through what he was doing. He talked and talked and found that, although it was very difficult to finally describe his hours looking at pornographic materials and masturbating, it was also a relief to let it out. When Father Jim asked him a couple of questions about it, it was clear to Paul that he wasn't shocked or disgusted.

They talked for a long time, and Paul found himself sharing a lot of worries he hadn't even thought about before. Father Jim suggested that Paul use half the hours that he had been spending on porn sites and masturbating to go for walks with Sheila after supper and to participate in morning Mass once a week. Paul agreed to come back in two months and jokingly said that now he would have to duck out the side door after Mass. Father Jim suggested that he come out the front door instead and introduce Sheila. Paul began to think that things were going to be all right after all.

In reconciliation, difficult or not so difficult, we find that we're not alone. In opening ourselves to God and to another person, we find ourselves experiencing God's mercy in the way we know best: through another person. In the priest's acceptance and compassion, we find Christ's hand on our shoulder. We find Jesus' heartfelt patience in the priest's quiet listening. We find ourselves gently held, challenged and deeply forgiven in an interaction between two persons that unfolds endlessly in the heart of God.

CHAPTER EIGHT

The Absolute Hardest Part

W_{hen} you celebrate the sacrament of reconciliation, you get to have a deeply personal experience of God's abundant mercy and forgiveness. It feels great. You start making changes here and there in your life, seeing progress, experiencing the freedom of being more and more honest with yourself. It's wonderful. You really like it.

Eventually, however, the day comes when you come to a horrible realization. Maybe you listen to the homily one Sunday and, for the first time, you really get the message. Maybe you pray the Lord's Prayer, and you stop to think about the words. Maybe you're reading Scripture and you suddenly realize:

> *We all have to forgive each other.*
> *All the time.*
> God mercifully forgives us. We have to forgive other people.
> Uh-oh.

If you're anything like me, you will immediately begin to try to figure out just who this might, and more importantly, might not, include. "Certainly," you will think to yourself, "this could not mean my miserable brother-in-law who got drunk and wrecked the boat and never even paid us back for the damage?" You will make lists of others that you don't have to forgive, usually because they were terribly wrong. Persons who have harmed, abused and exploited you will top the list, followed shortly by people who have taken advantage of you or your family, those who constantly put you down at work, those who are just nasty for no reason, those who have wrecked parts of your life, treated you unfairly and taken what's yours. Having made the list of those whom no reasonable God would expect you to forgive, you'll get on with the work of forgiving those that you can forgive more or less easily. "Sure," you'll think magnanimously, "Roger and Theresa never did send a wedding present, even though they sure didn't hesitate to guzzle free drinks at the reception two years ago, but I can forgive them!" So you'll forgive ol' Roger and Theresa, even send them a Christmas card this year. You'll forgive your wife for never getting you a Valentine's Day gift, and for telling her friends about how self-conscious you are about going bald, and for never, ever, ever, in twelve years of marriage, not even once saying, "thank you," for anything. You'll forgive your son for marrying a woman with a pierced nose and for moving six hundred miles away. You'll forgive your husband for getting you a leaf blower for your anniversary and then acting as though you could never possibly figure out how to use it without his constant expert supervision. You'll forgive the coworker who constantly takes credit for your work and who never chips into the coffee account. You'll forgive your sister who just took all of your mother's good china after she died without even asking the rest of the family. You'll forgive the guy who cuts you off in traffic. You may even forgive your pastor for his many transgressions.

After this little flurry of forgiving, you'll be feeling quite saintly. You'll be pleased to note that you now forgive more quickly and easily. You forgive people who don't even know they've offended you. Sometimes, you find yourself pontificating about the importance of forgiveness, how being able to forgive has changed your life, how forgiveness can be the main path to healing in all our lives. You'll give advice about forgiveness. Heck, you'll even entertain ideas about giving workshops about forgiveness or writing books about it. In short, you will become insufferable on this topic.

At this point you must do three things:

1. Talk to your confessor about pride.

2. Do the real work of forgiveness in your life.

3. Realize that step number 2 will take, more or less, the rest of your life.

We all have to face the fact that the Lord's Prayer does not say, "and forgive us our trespasses as we forgive some of those who trespass against us." Apparently, this was not an oversight on Jesus' part.

The idea of forgiving people who have physically abused us, who have killed our family members, who have cost us our jobs, who have wrecked our homes and stolen our possessions makes most of us want to throw up. We all have people in our lives that we cannot even think about forgiving without getting our guts into a horrible twist. Sometimes, especially in our families, an act that on the surface appears quite small has enormous meaning and leads to disproportionately great hurt. The matter of a wedding present can lead to painful chasms in family relationships that last through generations. In fact, in many of these cases, we have resolved never to forgive these people, vehemently and often. We say, "I will *never* forgive him. No matter if he comes crawling to me on his knees, begging and pleading! *Never! Nothing* he can say or do can change this!"

As Catholics, we regularly hear about the importance of forgiveness in homilies on Sunday. The reason for this is that Jesus' life and teaching were absolutely packed with examples and stories about forgiveness. His first words on the cross were about forgiveness. He called us, constantly and often, to forgive each other. This is another one of those things that we can't squirm away from, no matter how much we want to. Fortunately, in addition to hearing about it at Mass, we can read all about it in the Bible and we can talk about it in Scripture study group. There are plenty of books and tapes about forgiveness by thoughtful writers, and most parish retreats will spend at least a little time encouraging us to reflect on those areas of our lives where we need to exert forgiveness.

Lucky for you, I am still in the kindergarten of forgiveness myself, unlike the learned authors mentioned above, so I'm not going to try to give you any hot tips about it. This is a book about reconciliation, though, and so here are my ideas about how the sacrament of reconciliation can help us out:

1. Try to identify a part of your life where lack of forgiveness is a problem and talk about it in confession. The idea here is to at least acknowledge that you haven't forgiven someone. This doesn't mean that you have to say that you want to forgive them, only that you recognize that you aren't doing it at the moment.
2. Talk to the priest about what you think forgiving this person would mean. A lot of us have pretty confused ideas about this, and it helps to know that forgiveness doesn't necessarily mean being best friends with someone who has hurt us terribly.
3. Acknowledge in your prayer that, at the moment, you are quite incapable of forgiving this person.
4. Tell God that you are willing to have your heart changed about this.
5. Think about that person when you are asking for God's forgiveness.

Keep in mind that this isn't some kind of magic formula: just keep doing it and poof! instant forgiveness. It's more like you just keep doing it and it just keeps being painful and sometimes you get angry even thinking about it, and you get sick of looking at it and talking about it, and you think up ways to try to avoid it, and sometimes you just refuse to think about it for months, and you get irritated with your confessor if he asks about it and, mostly, you hang onto un-forgiveness for dear life. Eventually, though, you're going to forgive. It probably will surprise you when you do.

Here's an example:

Harrison's first memory of his mother was of being pushed out of her way as he tried to show her some coloring projects. All the rest of his memories are about her putting him down, not with yelling, but with one cutting remark after another, until she died when he was twenty-nine.

> *"You're just not that smart, are you, Harrison? I suppose you could be retarded."*
> *"Just cut those bangs off. Really, he's not much to look at, anyway."*
> *"You're a little sissy, aren't you? Pewling and whining like a girl. Disgusting!"*
> *"It's not much of a job, but I guess it's all you can expect."*

To make things worse, his mother was much admired in their town, both in her job as a manager at the bank and for her many volunteer projects. People would say to him, "Oh, I know your mother—what a wonderful woman! She really helped us out a few years ago." His father was a kind, responsible and equally successful man who enjoyed spending time with Harrison, but who had no idea that his wife was treating their son in this way. He thought that she maybe was not as warm as she might be and possibly not as interested in parenting as he was, but always supported her and loved her.

Now, at thirty-five, married and with two children of his own, after five years of therapy, Harrison finds himself at a parish retreat, sobbing his guts out after a talk about forgiveness and healing, realizing that he has to find some way to forgive his mother. Instead, he wishes she were still alive so that he could yell and scream at her, make her feel like the worm that she told him he was and somehow make her suffer even more than she did when she was dying from lung cancer. He realizes that he's got a big problem and that more therapy probably isn't the answer.

In reconciliation, he assures Father Paul that he knows that he is supposed to forgive his mother, but that he will never be able to. He's surprised to find Father Paul nodding in agreement but not saying much of anything. Eventually, Father Paul asks him why he would want to forgive his mother anyway, and Harrison talks about how he doesn't want to at all, but thinks that, as a Christian, he should. Father Paul nods some more, and at the end, asks Harrison if he thinks he could say a Hail Mary, for his mother. Harrison agrees to give it a try. Later, in the church, he does say a Hail Mary for his mother, but doesn't feel much different.

Things go on in this vein for months. A year and a half, actually. Harrison celebrates reconciliation in Lent and Advent and a couple of other times a year. He talks about how he will never be able to forgive his mother, but he has other things on his mind, as well. Father Paul ups the ante in the penance department a little so that Harrison is now saying a Hail Mary for his mother before Mass every Sunday.

One Saturday morning, Father Paul is helping Harrison spread new gravel on the walkway around the church, when Harrison says, "My mother's dead." Father Paul leans on his shovel for a bit, looking at Harrison, and nods like he always does. "Yup," he says, "for years, now," and Harrison feels something shifting in his heart. For Harrison, this was the beginning of forgiveness. It took another year of talking, and prayer, quite a few Hail Mary's and even more tears before he felt that he had actually forgiven his mother. He doesn't talk about it much now, but he sleeps better, and he never stops telling his kids, his wife, his father, his co-workers, his friends, clerks in the store, Father Paul, delivery persons and pretty much anyone he has contact with, how wonderful they are.

When Really Bad Things Have Happened to You

Some of the forgiving that we have to do can stem from horrible events and abuse. Maybe you've been raped. A family member has been killed. A friend has been tortured and mutilated. Many of us left the faith at times like these, feeling abandoned by God, not even sure that there is a God, certain that no God worth loving would allow such horrors to occur. We struggle with pain, alienation and rage. As we struggle with the absolutely repugnant idea of forgiveness under these circumstances, we sometimes come face to face with an even more distressing realization: we have to ask for forgiveness for ourselves, as well.

As we progress far enough to recognize that God is in our life now and always has been, we are confronted with our own, very human, weakness and failing. When times get tough, we do not always distinguish ourselves by spiritual courage and steadfastness. We not only turn away from God, but we push him out the door, throw rocks at him on the way out, and call him angry names once the door is triple locked and chained. We promise never to call on him again, except in contempt and hatred.

It's difficult while we are stuggling with the terrible idea of forgiving someone who has hurt us in an unspeakable way also to contend with our own need for forgiveness. As victims of such injury, we may have experienced a certain solicitude on the part of others around this event and have been reassured that what happened is not our fault. Perhaps we have had to bolster ourselves to deal with difficult legal proceedings, even aggressively to assert our rights in such matters. It's painful to acknowledge the ways that we, also, have failed spiritually during such times.

Usually, it's not possible for most of us to think of forgiving the person who hurt us for several months or even years after the event. Sometimes some of us can do it, especially if we've been very conscious of Christ in our lives in the years before. Most of us, though, will experience a period of un-forgiveness that corresponds with the pain and anger about what happened. It's not until we heal quite a bit that we can think about forgiveness. It's not until we've spent some time thinking about the need to forgive the person who hurt us that we can begin to recognize our own need to beg God's forgiveness for ourselves. This is something that we can bring to reconciliation.

· Try talking about the ways that you turned away from God, what you said, what you did and didn't do.

· Talk about the ways that you actively pushed God out of your life.

· Think back and talk about any ways that you think God might have been caring for you or calling you during this time, even when you couldn't see God or hear God.

· Talk about how it is that you became aware of and able to turn to God again. Why are you looking toward God in this sacrament?

· In prayer, be especially open to God's merciful love when you ask for forgiveness. This is a time to be particularly aware of the enfolding, embracing, very personal love that God rushes to offer us.

· Make sure that you have a good handful of tissues ready because you are going to sob like a baby.

When the Person That You Have to Forgive Is a Priest
Priests, we have come to discover, are not perfect. Some of us have been hurt by priests, sometimes unintentionally, sometimes intentionally and, occasionally, very badly. Some of us left Catholicism because of such hurts, large and small. Upon returning to Catholicism, we find ourselves in the very awkward position of turn-

ing toward the sacrament of reconciliation and recognizing with dismay that the person celebrating this sacrament with us is . . . a priest.

There is no way around this. You are going to have to accomplish a very particular kind of forgiveness. Fortunately, you don't have to do it all at once, and pretty much every parish priest has worked with at least a few people in your exact position. Here are some things to try or to keep in mind:

· Remind yourself that this priest is not the one who hurt you.

· Get to know your priest a little bit—go to a Scripture study group, work on a committee, listen to his homilies. This helps you see him as a person with his own strengths and weaknesses, quirks and interests. Maybe you'll find a person who tells corny jokes, who worries about his blood pressure, who's a recovering alcoholic, who's a published poet, a fanatical baseball nut, a novice violinist or an expert bridge player. Chances are good that the real priest will be a person that you can talk with, unlike the priest of memory.

· Make an appointment just to talk. Maybe you'll talk about past history and maybe you won't. If you're returning to Catholicism, no doubt there's plenty to talk about. Don't be too surprised if you find yourself blurting it all out right then and there. By the time most of us get to this point, past history is like a tidal wave all blocked up in us. It helps that most parish priests are extremely good listeners and make it easy for us to say what has to be said. You might even find that this conversation turns into a celebration of the sacrament of reconciliation, and you'll leave the office stunned, relieved and exhilarated.

· Talk about reconciliation and the difficulty of confessing to a priest, when it was a priest who hurt you. The priest will talk with you about that and try to help you see that, in reconciliation, you are turning, with the priest, to a merciful, loving God. Maybe you'll talk about the saving power of Christ in all of it and how his hand will not leave your shoulder in this sacrament.

· If you were sexually or physically abused by a priest, you might want to talk about other issues. Would you prefer not to be touched? Is there a way that the door to the office can be left open? How will you both handle it if you cry? Would it work out better if you sat in a pew in the church for reconciliation? Try to talk about these details in advance. Eventually, you'll find that these things don't matter any more, but at first, it's better to be conversational about them rather than act as though they don't exist. On the other hand, realize that there's a limit to what's realistic. If you find that you have to have absolute control over every tiny detail, chances are good that you're not quite ready, yet, and it would be better to wait.

· Focus on the present and what you're there for. You're turning to God to ask for his forgiveness and healing. You're about to celebrate a very powerful, meaningful, personal sacrament, and this priest is here to help you do that, now. This is not therapy—it is not about the relationship or process between you and the priest alone. It's about God and your relationship with God. If you keep this in mind, it clarifies things considerably.

· Pray.

· Acknowledge that maybe one of the sins that you have to confess is lack of forgiveness of the priest who hurt you.

· Realize that the priest sitting across from you is probably at least a little nervous about doing or saying something that is going to upset you or make everything worse. He has probably prayed to the Holy Spirit to help him out in a big way here. It wouldn't hurt if you gave him a little help yourself. In doing so, you will remind yourself that, after all, we are brothers and sisters struggling to repair and maintain our relationship with God, together.

Bad things happen to all of us. We live in an imperfect world, a world with sickness, death, pain of every imaginable kind. We hurt one another, sometimes grievously. As Catholics, we have in the sacrament of reconciliation a sure way to forgiveness and healing, and an ever-present reminder of our Lord's call to us to forgive one another. As we turn to God's mercy and open ourselves to the possibility of forgiving others, we further our own conversion, sometimes in sweeping ways.

Here in Maine, lakes and rivers freeze over in winter, and the topic of when the ice will go out is a matter for lively discussion for people living on the shores. The process of forgiveness can be like the ice going out in our hearts. Sometimes, we are frozen in a long winter of un-forgiveness. No water flows on the surface, but the currents below are icy, dark and treacherous. The ice layer is thick and durable, insulated by snow, crunchy underfoot, with some long stretches of glare ice. As we begin to think about forgiveness, God's radiating love warms the ice, but at first, all that melts is the snow on the surface. Occasional storms simply replace the snow, but as we progress, as spring moves toward summer, the warmth gets stronger, the sun shines longer, the snow storms are over.

One day, there is a huge resounding "crack!" in the ice, an explosion, a cannon shot, and we think, "This is it! Ice out!" Usually, though, this is just the first sign that something big is going to happen. The ice shifts a little and settles back, freezing into a new, less stable pattern. The surface is marked by the jagged edges of sheets of ice, with slushy water seeping up through the cracks. If there's a cold spell, the ice will stay in this new, dangerous formation for days. But spring progresses inevitably toward summer, as God's love relentlessly warms the ice in our hearts. One day we suddenly find the river rushing heedlessly for the ocean, with huge gouts of slush and big chunks of ice, dirty and packed with gravel underneath, full of sticks, old fishing gear, and the ragged pelts and bones of small animals. We didn't cause it, we didn't even know when it started, we just watched and waited, knowing that it absolutely was going to happen. We turn, and find the water coursing through the river, and through our hearts, wild, unimpeded and full of air. Everything about us has changed and will continue to change, often in unexpected ways. We lift our faces toward the sun and bask in the warmth of God's boundless mercy and love.

CHAPTER NINE

So What Now?

Some people have probably read this far and are saying, "Well, I've been going to confession for twenty-five years and it's nothing like this! I just say my sins, he gives me a penance and absolution and I'm out of there!" Some are saying, "Well, this is just fine for you, but I'm not doing it! No way." For the few that might be saying, "Well, maybe it's not as bad as I thought. Father Mark seems like he's been around . . . ," here are some ideas:

1. Your own parish is the best place to start. If you haven't been to Mass in a while, go. Pay attention to the homily while you're at it.

2. Make an appointment just to talk with the priest, to get to know each other a little.

3. Make an appointment to talk about reconciliation. You don't have to do it, just talk about it.

4. When in doubt, pray. Actually, you can pray even when not in doubt. You can read readymade prayers and think about them. You can read parts of the Bible (try Psalm 139) and think about them. You could say the Lord's Prayer slowly and think about it.

You can just talk to God. Or you can just sit quietly with God and not read anything or say anything and just listen.

5. Or, you can say to yourself, "Hey! How hard can it be?," make an appointment, go in, sit down and say, "Well, Father, I haven't had reconciliation in twenty years and I have no clue what to do and I'm as nervous as can be, so can you help me out here?"

Ours is a merciful God, a God who tracks us down and stirs our hearts, who longs for our coming home, who welcomes us with gentleness and love. Take a minute to think about why you even picked up this book, of what you might be searching for, of what your own longing might be. Maybe you have already begun turning toward reconciliation, toward that continual Coming Home that we share with all Christians.